THE BACKWARD LOOK

By SUSANNE RIKE MACDONALD

Three Score Years and Then . . .
("By Anne MacFarland")

The Backward Look

The Backward Look

MEMOIRS OF

Susanne Rike MacDonald

*Tische Mason,
With profound appreciation,
from Susanne MacDonald.
May 20, 1957.*

Exposition Press   •   New York

EXPOSITION PRESS INC., 386 Fourth Avenue, New York 16, N.Y.

FIRST EDITION

To my parents

DAVID & SALOME RIKE

Contents

Prologue

Why should a second book of memoirs follow *Three Score Years and Then* . . . written under the pen name of Anne MacFarland? Here are the answers:

The publisher urges that the second book would increase the sale of the first.

More than a few eminent clergymen, college professors and authors have written, "Give us more memoirs." These tributes have been received by the author with surprise and gratitude.

However, the deeply motivating answer lies in earnest requests from many readers, wholly unknown to the author before she received their letters—letters which also brought surprise and joy, and at the same time a deep humbleness of spirit. For these letters tell that difficult personal problems have been solved by the opening of a window into hitherto sealed hearts and minds, open for the first time to the difficult, yet challenging experience of honest *self-appraisal*, and the letting in of God-given sunlight of faith, hope and love.

SUSANNE RIKE MACDONALD

CHAPTER I

My Home

In my girlhood home lived my father, my mother, my brother, and myself, also "Aunt Ella," the high school teacher to whom my mother offered a temporary home and who remained with us twenty-three years. Also the "hired girl," the washerwoman (who received one dollar for a full day's work), the man of all work, and an occasional yard-man.

I can still recall the black skin and the half-withdrawn, half-wishful look on the face of one occasional yard-man. Absorbed in our own affairs, we never became aware of his longing for the understanding he never received. He was the great Negro poet, Paul Laurence Dunbar, who died so young, unknown and unrecognized. After his death a full measure of fame and praise were his—for a time. Yet he still lives on! His name as a poet, together with the dates of his birth and death, occupy two lines in the Biographical Notes in the latest edition of Webster's *Collegiate Dictionary*!

Our three-story house was built of brick. We lived at the dawn of an era of progress, when gas still feebly lighted our rooms until the experiment with electric lights proved a success; when the installation of a telephone was an experiment even more dubious; a wooden box fastened to the wall at the extreme end of the long dining room contained the *incredible*, many, many footsteps away.

Our front door opened into an unimpressive hallway from

which, by a sharp turn to the left, the "front stairs" climbed abruptly until they curved to reach the second floor. The space below was just wide enough for an umbrella-stand, and an all-purpose piece of furniture with hat-racks and a large mirror. To the right, near the front door, was the entrance into the "front parlor," an ample room dignified by a bay window facing the street and by tall windows on either side of a marble fireplace. A large, square room, originally intended as a nursery, became the "back parlor" when the dividing wall was demolished and the two became one spacious room. Yet to the immediate family, because each area had a different function, each retained its identity. The "front parlor" was used exclusively for "callers" and for formal entertainment. The "back parlor" was where my brother and I entertained our friends.

We not only had a front staircase; we had a "back-stairs" as well. This area of our home had been badly planned. The "back parlor," the dining room and the kitchen opened onto a small square space inadequate for the traffic which passed through it. Abruptly from it, a steep stairs gave access to the "hired girl's room" and a short hall which led to the narrow, long hall of the second floor. At the end of this hall, above the dining room, was the one bathroom, the one toilet in the house. Looking back in this year of 1956 when, in even the smallest new homes, the essential feature is ample plumbing, I cannot understand why my father and I, with our zeal for "modernizing," failed to realize the utter inadequacy of plumbing in our home.

In the "back parlor" a square Steinway piano was installed. Memories released from oblivion, like the opening of Pandora's box, come alive. I see myself, a tearful, rebellious six-year-old, practicing scales while my determined mother, her knitting needles flashing, sat behind me for one hour each day. She felt keenly the lack of musical talent in herself; hopefully she recognized the awakening of musical talent in her daughter. The development of that talent is another chapter in my story.

The "front hall" reached past the hat-rack and the umbrella-stand to the "sitting room," the real focus of our family life. Opening from it onto a side-porch was the door through which we came and went. The front door was for visitors. In the sitting room every morning after breakfast we had family prayers. Each of us had our own Bible, and as mother read from her church-paper the lesson for the day, we learned to know the books of the Bible in their proper order, stumbling only over the Minor Prophets. As the years passed and my brother and I had overnight guests, they were also handed Bibles, and often, not knowing First Chronicles from First Corinthians, they suffered agonies of embarrassment vainly trying to find the place.

Mother was a lively, fun-loving girl of eighteen when she married my father, thirteen years her senior. As was the custom in that year of 1855, she became at once a matron, wearing when she went forth a bonnet with "strings" demurely tied beneath her chin. She wore her masses of lustrous brown hair tightly wound into a coil on top of her head. At that time her hair reached below her knees. When she died, at the age of eighty-four, two heavy braids of hair only touched with gray reached below her waist.

As a result of his marriage, father was converted and joined the United Brethren Church (an off-shoot of the German Reformed), in which his wife's forebears had played so prominent a part and in which, as the years went by, he and my mother became known and honored throughout the entire denomination.

Mother had a mind of rare intelligence and leadership. She deplored the fact that she had had but one year at a small "Female Academy." It was Aunt Ella, the inestimable influence for education in our home, who persuaded mother to take the Chautauqua course of study. Mother responded eagerly and after four years she went to Chautauqua, where she graduated with honors.

My brother and I went together to a public grade school. He was sixteen months older than I, but whereas I had "skipped" two grades, he had lagged behind. The school we attended had as its principal and vice-principal two old-maid sisters who hid their own incompetence behind a bluster of fussiness.

My brother lost interest; his entire young body sagged. It was a time of crisis for him. Aunt Ella quietly used her influence to have him transferred to another district school, whose principal was an alert and highly capable man. With keen insight and sharp discipline he brought my brother out of the doldrums and taught him that most valuable of lessons, the value of his own mind and soul.

Not long afterward, Aunt Ella recognized that we needed her room. She shed a few tears, in which we joined, built a very dwellable house, sent for her old-maid sister, and found a freedom and happiness she had not enjoyed before.

As the years passed and father's business prospered, our house was modernized in the fashion of that day. The wall-to-wall carpets were replaced by highly polished hardwood floors strewn with colorful oriental rugs. A wide opening into the "front parlor" increased the dignity of the hall. Father and I conspired to widen the opening from the sitting room into the dining room, sliding doors affording privacy when desired. We also conspired to panel the long dining room in shiny golden oak, and, deaf to mother's pleas, we replaced her handsome black walnut furnishings with shiny golden oak. The sitting room remained the same except for larger bookcases needed for our growing library. I have wondered what became of the golden oak. It has vanished, but three of the precious black walnut dining room chairs are still in use in my home today.

Although my father will appear again and again in my story, I shall relate here the scene of his death, for it was at this period in the backward look that he died after a brief illness at the age of seventy-two. It might have been the death-bed scene of some patriarch of medieval times. Our church pastor and three leading elders of the church sat at one side of the room. Seated opposite the bed, my mother and brother clung to each other, drawing strength from an invisible Source. I sat close to my father at the head of his bed, moved beyond tears by this first contact with the mystery of death, awed by the indescribable peace upon his face.

One of the elders, a self-righteous man, spoke, "Are you sure, Brother David, that you are prepared to meet your Maker?"

Without moving, my father answered faintly, but firmly, "Of course I'm ready! I just hadn't thought it would come so soon!"

And thus he died.

CHAPTER II

The Proposals

It has been accepted as a fact that the majority of very old people are interested in the present only as it concerns themselves. They are quite forgetful of the immediate past. Old as I am, it is the adventure of the future that fascinates me; for I, too, am not concerned with the immediate past.

It is "the backward look" that brings into focus a lively teen-age girl. I have difficulty in recognizing her. Was I really that girl over half a century ago? Let me delve into her past. What shall I bring up? Take, for instance, my first proposal of marriage.

I see myself in the "front parlor" seated at one end of a davenport, a young man at the other end. He and his sister were in the same "crowd" to which I belonged. She was an intimate friend. He was what we called "heavy cake" and I had avoided him when possible.

On this memorable evening our chit-chat dragged. Suddenly he moved near to me and laid his hand over mine, his eyes—in which no ardor burned—fixed upon my face. Before I could withdraw my hand he said, "Of course, you are homely; but I must say you have qualities which win. I want you to marry me!"

"Marry *you*?" I exclaimed and laughed my scorn. He stared at me for a moment and then without a word he walked to the hall, picked up his hat and departed, unaware that he had left his revenge behind him.

I ran upstairs to my room, closed my door, switched on the lights and stood before my mirror to study my face.

"Of course, you are homely."

From that moment an inferiority complex took root and for too many years it bore its bitter fruit.

"Of course, you are homely!" I accepted his dictum, although I could not accept him!

Noah Webster defines "shavetail" (soldier's slang) as a "recently appointed second lieutenant, humorously so-called with allusion to the young unbroken army mules."

Tom Seldon was a farm boy with a burning ambition to win an appointment as a cadet to West Point Military Academy. Twice a day, five days a week, he walked nine miles to the Dayton High School and nine miles back to the farm, usually with a load of books under his arm. He was an apt student and he won his cadetship. Four years later, he graduated and he came to Dayton for a brief vacation before departing for his assignment, a remote army post out west where hostile Indians had recently massacred General Custer and his handful of troops.

I had just returned from a camping trip with my family and I found that everywhere Lieutenant Seldon was the main topic of conversation.

One evening, two young men who belonged to our "crowd" rowed another girl and myself up the river to a pleasant summer resort provided with an ample room for dancing, and soft drinks for refreshment. Tom Seldon was there in uniform; consequently, in the eyes of the girls at least, he outshone every other man in the room. On the way up the river, my friends had "briefed me" on the lieutenant.

"He brags!" they said. "He claims that he has yet to meet a girl he cannot kiss!" I had no desire to meet Tom Seldon!

He must have asked to be introduced to me. He not only was introduced; he asked for a dance. We had circled the room only once when he took advantage of our proximity in the waltz and embraced me. For a few steps I made no attempt to break away from him, then I stopped.

"It is very warm in here," I said. "Can't we go outside?"

I caught the gleam in his eyes, but side by side we walked to the door.

The look on my friends' faces expressed incredulity, amazement. "Has *she* fallen for him *too?*"

We walked beyond the light which shimmered from the hall. In the shadow was a log. "Let us sit here," I said.

He sat very close and put his arm around me. It was a bright moonlight night, and I could see his face. He could see mine, and what he saw there caused him suddenly to withdraw his arm.

"You have boasted," I began, "that you have yet to meet a girl you couldn't kiss. Well, you are meeting one now, and she isn't going to scream for help, although she has some friends in there who are itching for a fight with you. You have dishonored the great institution you've just graduated from. You've dishonored the uniform you have on. Let's go in. I hope that I shall never see you again!"

We had been outside not more than five minutes. When we re-entered the hall, something in his face restored my friends' confidence in me.

The next morning when I answered the doorbell, there stood Lieutenant Seldon with a large box of flowers under his arm and a hopeful look on his face. My impulse was to slam the door in his face. Perhaps I had punished him enough.

"May I please come in?" All his bravado had left him. "I must explain!"

Reluctantly I invited him to enter and I indicated a chair. "I've never met a girl like you before," he began. "All the time I was going to high school, I didn't have time for girls. And there at West Point . . ."

"Never mind the girls at West Point!" I interrupted. "Just why have you come here this morning?"

His face reddened, then became a little pale.

"You held up a mirror before me last night, and for the first time I saw myself as I really am. I couldn't sleep. I kept thinking what a blessing—what a God-given blessing—it would be to have a wife like you. No . . . *please* let me explain!" (I had half-arisen from my chair.) "I want to write to you and I hope you will answer my letters. It will be a very lonely place to which I am going. No, it isn't self-pity!" (I had raised my hand in protest.) "You don't believe it possible for a man to fall so deeply in love in so short a time. I don't believe there can be true love without respect. All I ask is: will you write to me? I don't mean will you answer *all* my letters. I may write to you every day. But *do* write! So that I'll know you just as I hope you'll learn to know me. Pray for me, please!"

With that, he suddenly arose and departed. He had not even touched my hand. For that I respected him. And he had not called attention to the flowers. Within a short time his letters began coming. He wrote interestingly about the remote post to which he had been assigned. Occasionally he sent me little gifts from the army post. One handsome gift was of solid gold, two sabers crossed. I was delighted with the pin and wrote to tell him so. Delighted, that is, until I learned its significance. And here I must digress to tell how I learned.

My mother was giving an afternoon reception. She agreed with the senior Oliver Wendell Holmes' description of an afternoon *tea*: "Giggle, gabble, gobble, git!" Mrs. Custer, widow of the murdered general, earning her livelihood by giving talks at clubs and at social functions, was to speak at my mother's reception; and as Mrs. Custer was a guest in our home, I was privileged to talk with that very gracious lady.

I was wearing the crossed sabers. "Oh, you are engaged to an Army man! Let me congratulate you both!" she exclaimed with delight.

"Oh, no!" I protested. "I don't even like him very much, but he is so lonely that I write just to cheer him up."

Mrs. Custer's face grew grave. "You don't know what you are doing, my dear. It is a tradition in the army that when a girl accepts the crossed sabers pin, she is accepting the suitor. In the service, it is even more binding than an engagement ring."

How could I return the pin after my enthusiastic acceptance of it? There was a drive for gold at that time. It served a useful purpose.

But my letters to Tom Seldon were much farther apart and much more impersonal. My brother, Frank, and I had a more intimate relationship than with our busy mother and father. Frank knew all about Tom Seldon. At first he was inclined to chide me. "You're leading him on!" he accused. But when I convinced him that I didn't really like Tom Seldon and only wrote to him because he needed a friend, my brother became concerned about the lieutenant. Then there came a letter so full of despair that I answered quite frankly that he was destroying our friendship rather than strengthening it.

There came a quick reply. Tom threatened suicide. My brother didn't know the male animal as well as I did. He took the threat very seriously. He became more and more concerned. And when two weeks went by without a letter, then a month, and then five weeks, Frank declared, "I really ought to go out there. He needs help."

"That long journey?" I exclaimed. "He's like King Saul, sulking in his tent."

Frank was only partially convinced. "We'll wait a while."

Finally, at the end of ten weeks, I received a letter. It was brief, but to the point.

"I am writing to tell you that three weeks ago I was married, and my dearest wish is to see my little Bessie and you together." Signed: "Your happy friend and well-wisher, Tom Seldon."

CHAPTER III

Studies Abroad

At the fairground outside the city of Hamilton, Ohio, on a hot summer day, the Kumlers and their connections were holding a family reunion. Outstanding in this large assembly was a handsome young woman, Katherine Woodman by name, from whom my father was asking a favor.

"I understand you are going abroad to study singing. Susie, here, wants very much to study abroad. Would you be willing to let her go with you?"

I dreaded her reply. She had been at the New England Conservatory of Music when I was there. She was a hard-working student, aware of my all-too-obvious waste of time. We had nothing in common. I had seldom seen her. Now her tall figure became more rigidly erect as she answered my father.

"There are two girls and eight boys in our family. My mother is dead. My father has sent two of my brothers to college. My sister escaped years ago. She *worked* her way through college; now she's principal of a high school. I told my father that I'm not going to stay home and fry mush for him and the boys the rest of my life. We've had quite a battle. He's given me a thousand dollars and told me not to expect anything more." She paused a moment. "I *can't* be responsible for your daughter. Of course, if she would be willing to *work* . . ." She made an impatient gesture. "My answer must be *no!*"

Father looked at me. I was praying, and he knew it.

"Kate," he said, "I'll give you five hundred dollars if you'll let Susie go with you. She is a responsible girl. All I ask of you is that you see she gets a good teacher, and that you find a good place where you can live together."

Katherine's eyes shone. It was not altogether because of the money, although that was important. She was ten years older than I. She would be my big sister.

On a certain day in August, Katherine and I sailed on the French liner, *La Touraine*, bound for Le Havre. We were assigned to a table with five men, all foreigners. Katherine and I could speak only a few words in French, and those mispronounced. Only one of the men could speak English. He was the youngest in the group. He was from Switzerland and he made annual trips to sell the linens manufactured by his father. The shy little man at the head of the table to my right could speak some English, very brokenly. Kate and I sat with our backs to the dining room. The men were ahead of us; they had the best seats. Kate and I had never before been served by a waiter proffering food to us at our left side. We were all the more awkward because we were aware that our table-companions were laughing at our greenness.

It was the artichokes that broke the ice. Neither of us had ever seen an artichoke before. As the waiter held the platter, we felt five pairs of eyes watching. Then there was an outburst of laughter.

"You have taken only the sauce and left the 'choke.'" Mr. Switzerland laughed. "Let me demonstrate how to eat an artichoke!"

Because we could laugh with the five men, we were good companions for the remainder of the voyage. The quiet little man whispered to me, "I vill lent you my Bible!"

"Thank you; I have my own Bible. My friend also has hers."

We were good friends for the remainder of the voyage.

When we reached Paris, Kate and I had some important

problems to solve. At that time, the majority of American students lived in the Latin Quarter on the left bank of the Seine. Students of music were compelled to live on the right bank because of the widely scattered studios of music-teachers. Our most important errand was to find a permanent place in which to live. We were staying temporarily at a small hotel near the Arc de Triomphe. A kindly woman there recommended to us a pension kept by Mlle. Hommey, who at one time had been at the head of a large school for girls. She had prepared American girls for the Sorbonne. Lessons in French were included in her price.

We hired a cab and drove over to the Rue Lemercier to interview Mlle. Hommey and to appraise her pension. We were surprised and delighted with what we found inside the door that opened so abruptly off the street. Mlle. Hommey accepted us; we accepted her. We had found the ideal permanent home! It was in the Quartier des Batignolles, a truly French quarter uninvaded by foreigners, inhabited by small tradesmen, the butcher, the baker, the candlestick-maker. Opposite our door was a little shop where the proprietor sold fuel and wine. Here the women came for charcoal, carrying it away in baskets, sometimes in their aprons. Farther down the street was a butcher's shop with a horse's head over the door, indicating that only horse-meat was sold there. Often a large carcass gaily adorned with paper roses hung by the door with the interesting inscription which read (translated in English), MULE! FIRST QUALITY! We were assured that our meats did not come from that shop, but that many of the thick, juicy steaks we enjoyed came from America.

Mlle. Hommey, in spite of her age and almost total loss of eyesight, loved the world and its pleasures. She was absolved from fasting and she sat down to her food with no thought of religious form. Mlle. Aline, who had been assistant at the school for girls, with downcast eyes and a reverence that rebuked our own attitude, crossed herself and sat apart to eat a frugal meal.

In Mlle. Hommey's salon there was a grand piano and

handsome pieces of furniture upholstered in worn, but still beautiful fabrics which would have made them collectors' items in our homeland. A second room opened from the salon. It was there that Mlle. gave us our lessons. Beyond was a garden with gravelled walks, its privacy secured by trees and tall shrubs.

Once a week, Monsieur l'Abbé LeRis came to dine. Always, a number of friends were invited to meet him. None could speak English. M. l'Abbé had been a pupil of Delsarte. With his round, ruddy face, his flowing soutane, his never-quiet, ever-gesticulating white hands, he was the center and life of the party. What an easy, jolly, careless spiritual leader! How often Mlle. Hommey had to interrupt some story of his by an admonishing touch of her foot under the table and a warning glance toward *les Américaines!*

Katherine and I had two rooms on the second floor. We rented a piano. We were ready now for our all-important interview with Mme. Marchesi, the most famous voice teacher of her time. She granted us an appointment and met us at the door. It was August, and every piece of furniture in the suite of rooms through which we passed was hidden beneath coveralls of linen tailored to fit. Madame led us to a music room upstairs, where there was a grand piano and . . . Madame with her questions!

She addressed us in French, but quickly changed to flawless English.

"How many languages do you speak?" she asked.

We answered, "Only English."

She corrected us. "You speak only American! You do *not* speak English correctly. In France, a young lady to *be* a lady must be fluent in five languages. I myself speak eight. Now, let me hear you sing."

When we had finished the test, she addressed me. "You sing much better than your friend. When my classes begin in September, I can do much for both of you."

"*Classes?*" I asked. "Do you teach only *classes?*"

"I teach no other way," she replied tersely.

Her method seemed clear enough to me. Undoubtedly she was a great teacher; but by humbling the student at the beginning of her course, she could claim later all the credit for the pupil's improvement.

Another famous teacher, formerly the greatest soprano of her time, agreed to give me lessons. The American dollar was desirable. From my point of view, she was not. What to do?

Then, I recalled a name that had occurred in a novel I read on shipboard: Monsieur Wartel, a great singing-master. Was he fictional or was he real?

He was *very* real! I became his pupil at once. He spoke no English. His accompanist spoke it fluently; but he taught with a ruler. Yes, an ordinary ruler! With a tap of his ruler on my lower jaw, he taught me how to open my mouth, how to breathe, where to direct the tone.

One day at the end of my lesson, as I was about to leave the studio for my return to our pension, the accompanist exclaimed, "You Americans! You can walk the streets alone because you *are* Americans! A French girl could never find a husband were she to go about without a chaperone. A friend of mine has a daughter seventeen years old who has never even crossed the street to mail a letter unless her mother or a maid goes with her. The most beautiful and intelligent girl I know is an object of deep sympathy because she has no *dot* and must work for her livelihood. No Frenchman would be that generous!"

By a strange coincidence, as I approached the dingy quarter of Les Batignolles that morning and had just turned a corner, a young man fell into step beside me.

He was an apparition from another world—faultlessly attired in a formal cutaway morning coat, striped trousers, a silk top hat, jauntily carrying a walking-stick under his arm.

With a smile, but without a word, he fell into step beside me and bent toward me, gazing into my eyes. Without a falter in my step, my eyes looked through and beyond his. *He wasn't there!* Thus we walked for an entire block. My eyes never faltered. We came to the corner. Without a word, he removed his hat, and with it in his hand (and respect in his eyes) he made a low bow and walked swiftly away.

How unpredictable can the female of the species be! With my love of adventure, I wondered, half regretfully, what would have happened had I let him know I knew he was there?

Kate waited a month, then impressed by the improvement Monsieur Wartel had made in my singing, she too became his pupil. At the end of ten months she went to Mme. Marchesi again, wanting the prestige of her name, yet fearful lest she be recognized. Mme. Marchesi did not remember her. She fell in love with her . . . but that is another story. Katherine had learned a great deal in those ten months. She spoke French accurately. She had acquired self-confidence. Wartel had brought forth all the richness of her deep contralto voice. After a few months, Mme. Marchesi used her influence to have Katherine join a group leaving for a concert tour in South Africa.

A deep affection had ripened between Katherine and me. After she had gone, I decided that oratorio was best suited to my voice, and I crossed over to London to study under George Henschel. It was he who taught me how to speak English without the Ohio twang.

I wanted to get as much experience as possible. I decided to have some lessons from Paola Tosti. He made an appointment and requested that I bring a song so that he might hear my voice. He lived far away from the lodging George Henschel had found for me. I had to hurry to catch a bus. I cut my finger. There was no Band-Aid in those days. I hastily tied up the bleeding finger, picked up a song by a little-known American composer, and just caught the bus! By the time I reached Paola Tosti's rooms, the rag around my finger was black with London's polluted air. When Signor Tosti saw the name of the song I had brought and its composer, he refused to play the accompaniment. The dirty rag bobbed up and down. If I put any feeling into the song, it was disgust with myself. Paola Tosti wrote that he would accept me as a pupil. I should have preserved his letter! I did not go back. I was ill.

I returned to Paris and went to the hotel where mother was to meet me. We were to go to Italy together. My good American doctor ordered complete rest for me.

Mother's great desire was to see Rome. I sent her to two remarkable old ladies who had lived at Mlle. Hommey's pension and who had become my dear friends. They met mother at the train and took her on a tour of Italy.

She wrote that when she went to the Roman Forum for the first time, she purposely went alone. She fell on her knees to thank God that she was permitted to see the place where the Apostle Paul spoke for his risen Christ.

After a rest of three weeks, I was permitted to go to Florence to meet mother and to consult an eminent American physician there. After a thorough examination, the doctor told my mother that I was in no condition to go on a sightseeing tour. I was ready to weep over the disappointment this would be to her, when I heard the doctor say, "I have just the place for a rest-cure. Do you know Mainz?" He pronounced it "my aunts"; and from the puzzled look on mother's face, I knew that she was about to ask, *"Your aunts?"*

I intervened just in time! "Just where is Mainz, and how do we get there?"

He sent us to a pension at Bad Langen Schwalbach, where we remained for a month. During this quiet period, mother and I came to know and understand each other as never before.

Mother wore no wedding ring. Her finger had grown too large for it, and she had left it at home. The ladies at the pension looked somewhat askance. A woman with a grown daughter and no wedding ring? Mother found a little jewelry shop near by and bought a gold ring.

We rented two chairs in which we could recline and read out on a grassy slope a short distance from the pension. Soon the Britishers from another pension were occupying our chairs. Mother went back to the little shop. She had seen small American flags for sale there. She bought four, and we fastened them to our chairs. Thereafter the Britishers left them alone.

On our return trip to Paris, we went by steamboat down the river Rhine. Brother Frank had written, "On that ride down the river, drink a glass of Rudesheimer for me." The dining room of the steamer was below deck. It was hot and stuffy. The waiter refused to serve Rudesheimer wine by the glass. Mother ordered a bottle. It was a *very* tall bottle! Neither of us was accustomed to wine. Mother's ingrained habit of economy bade that the contents of that bottle should be consumed. She filled and refilled my glass and her own . . . and refilled!

"I must get on deck," I gasped.

She followed me. We sank into our chairs. My recollection of the castles on the Rhine is of large buildings now zigging, now zagging, but never a one standing erect and still!

CHAPTER IV

Vignettes

Noah Webster has defined a "vignette" as "a depiction in words, esp. one of a small or dainty kind."

1

In a recent news-picture of young Queen Elizabeth presiding at the picturesque ceremony of the Changing of the Guard, she was riding her horse "sidesaddle," wearing a long-skirted riding habit, a stiff silk hat perched upon her head.

In the long, long ago, clad exactly as was the young queen, I was riding a horse "sidesaddle" around and around a tanbark circle, learning how to sit erect, how to hold the reins and the crop. When my father decided I could manage a horse, he bought for me a young Kentucky five-gaited thoroughbred whom I named "Nobby," the slang word for "stylish." For Nobby was "stylish" in appearance and disposition. No one was permitted to ride him but myself. We soon understood each other. Could there have been a *female* Centaur? Nobby and I were usually of one mind, but I had control.

One bright spring morning we were passing down a quiet street, Nobby on three legs in one of his fanciest gaits. Suddenly there came an anxious voice; an elderly gentleman running down the steps of his house and calling, "Young lady!

Young lady! That is a very dangerous horse for you to ride!"

I laughed and waved my crop at him. The Centaur danced on!

2

In the long, long ago there were no movies, no night clubs, no television sets. A young man would come to call on me, and we just sat and talked. If he remained until 10:30, my father would appear in the doorway, watch in hand, and say with finality, "Young man, it's time to go!"

One evening there came a young man who bored me. After a while I began to needle him. The topic was: the kiss, and my abhorrence thereof. Finally his slow mind reached the conclusion that I *wanted* him to kiss me; and, in present-day slang, he made a pass at me. Quick as a flash I grabbed the brass-handled poker from beside the fireplace, whirled behind a large overstuffed chair, and brandished my weapon.

"You get out of this house," I commanded, "and never enter it again!"

He went.

3

Everett and I had been married a short year when we went to Chicago to attend my brother's wedding.

My husband could not afford to be away from his practice and he returned to Dayton the day after the wedding. I remained to spend four or five days with friends musically inclined. A young man of their acquaintance became a constant visitor during my stay. Perhaps I flirted with him a little, but to me and my host and hostess it was all innocent fun.

One night, a week after my return home, my husband was detained at his office. I was alone in the house. The doorbell rang. When I answered it and opened the door, there stood the young man from Chicago. He walked in with a possessive air about him as though there was no "Mrs." attached to my name. He frightened me! How was I to get rid of him?

If you pray quite earnestly, there will always be a way!

"This is prayer-meeting-night," I said, "and my husband is busy at his office. I don't like to go alone. Will you please go with me?"

Yes, he went to prayer-meeting and in complete silence he escorted me home. He waited until I had opened the door and then with a curt "good-night" he hurried away.

When I told Everett what had happened, he looked as though he felt rather sorry for the young man.

"You really took him to *prayer-meeting*?" he asked, and then he laughed. "Humph!" he said.

4

The graduation exercises of United Theological Seminary of Dayton, Ohio, were to be held in the capacious sanctuary of the United Brethren Church, to which my family belonged.

Each graduate was assigned ten minutes in which to preach a test sermon before he received his diploma. His name and the subject of his discourse were printed upon the programs distributed to the large audience.

Halfway down the lengthy program my name appeared: Vocal Solo by Miss Susie Rike . . . "Lord, I Am Weary, Cried My Soul!" How *could* I have chosen that title for my song? (Although personally it was painfully true.) To atone for my ineptitude I poured my very soul into the interpretation of my solo.

A week later, mother, father, my brother and I had just finished family prayer when the postman delivered the morning mail. I received an envelope addressed to me in an unfamiliar hand. I tore open the envelope and read the letter it enclosed.

DEAR MISS RIKE:

I am one of the recent graduates from United Theological Seminary. You may recall my name on the program. I heard you sing and I was deeply impressed by your character as that of a highly-cultured, Christian lady. I wish to correspond with you with the aim of becoming better acquainted, leading to the ultimate goal of matrimony. I have been assigned to a church where I am to receive a salary of $800.00 a year. . . .

At that point I waved the letter over my head and shouted with laughter. My brother seized the letter and read it aloud with mounting indignation.

"The nerve of him!" he exploded. "'Correspond with a view to matrimony'! If I knew where to find him I'd teach him a thing or two!"

Father's face had turned purple. I had never seen him look so angry. His eyes sought my mother's. His anger ebbed. "After all, he *is* a man of the cloth," he said.

Mother reached out her hand to me. "Give me the letter."

Reluctantly I obeyed. She took the letter and tore it in half.

"You were planning to have fun at this young man's expense," she said. "You would be showing more bad taste than he did. Why, not fifteen minutes ago in our Bible lesson for today, did we not read: 'Whoso keepeth his mouth and his tongue, keepeth his soul from troubles'? We shall have no more talk about this!"

5

An eminent psychiatrist has declared that an infant displays will-power the day it is born.

"Train up a child in the way he should go, and when he is old he will not depart from it" (Proverbs 22:6).

Who can measure the understanding of a six-year-old child, weeping rebellious tears one day because she must practice scales on the piano; then a week, perhaps a month later, so moved by a spiritual experience that it will remain with her the rest of her life. No matter how her nature may change superficially in the years to come, basically her nature will not be moved.

Our church was only two blocks up the street from our home; only two intersections to cross. There was no peril from traffic in those days. At the age of six I was permitted to go alone to attend a Bible class for children held one morning each week at the church. On one such morning, our porch thermometer registered ten degrees below zero. Mother saw to it that I was warmly clad, and she helped me push my hands into a brand-new pair of black kid gloves warmly interlined with fleece.

When the class was dismissed, I wept all the way home. I could find no handkerchief; I wiped my tears with my new black gloves. Mother was watching for me. When she opened the door, I flung myself into her arms, sobbing uncontrollably.

"My child!" exclaimed my mother, "what has happened? You have made your face black from your gloves. Come! Let me take them off and wash your face. Then tell me what has happened. Did some one hurt you?"

"Oh, no, Mama! I'm so happy! Teacher taught us to repeat what Jesus said: 'Suffer little children to come unto me and forbid them not, for of such is the Kingdom of Heaven!' And then Jesus said: 'If you don't accept God's Kingdom as a little child, you can never, never enter in.' Mama, that means me! Why didn't I ever know that before?"

CHAPTER V

Otterbein

We were at breakfast one morning, Father, Mother and I. Our guest was Dr. Sanders, President of Otterbein University. He came often to confer with my father, who was Chairman of Otterbein's Board of Trustees. Dr. Sanders had held a long conference with Father the night before. At the breakfast table he brought up another problem.

"We've enough money to pay an adequate salary for an instructor and leader of our excellent band; however, a number of our students are studying to become pastors. They want to learn to sing, so that they can lead their congregations in the singing of hymns." Dr. Sanders passed his cup for some more coffee and resumed: "As I say, we have enough to pay the band-leader, but we have absolutely nothing for a vocal teacher—a woman, probably. She would have to depend wholly upon what she could earn for herself." He shook his head unhopefully.

As he spoke, Opportunity knocked loudly at my door.

"I'll undertake the job!" I exclaimed.

Father was delighted; Mother was dubious. Could I undertake so responsible a position with the seriousness it demanded?

My father's pleasure over my acceptance of this position at Otterbein sprang from his deep-rooted interest in the college itself. He had begun life as a farm boy well-acquainted with hard work. He had little opportunity for an education until he was twenty-one years old. Then for a time he attended a private academy, working for his board and tuition. In a biographical sketch written after his death, the writer states that this venture into what was then regarded as "higher education" led him to venture into the commercial world. He secured a position in a general store for sixty dollars a year, plus room and board. Later he secured a position in a Dayton store at $110 a year. Out of this small salary he saved enough to start his own business. That was in 1853, when he was twenty-nine years old.

He acquired the use of good English by his study of the Bible, by careful reading of daily newspapers and the best of current magazines. Because of his lack of a college education in his own life, he became a staunch supporter of Otterbein. As an institution, it was a pioneer, even as the state of Ohio itself was on the frontier in 1872.

I have heard my father tell how several men on the staff at Otterbein approached him in his little dry goods store in Dayton one day and asked him for a gift of $5,000. "I haven't that kind of money to give," he told them, "but I promise you that if ever I am worth $50,000, you will get your $5,000. That was the first of many sacrificial gifts he and my mother made to the struggling institution; and that is why, as Chairman of the Board of Trustees, he was happy to have his daughter teach at Otterbein.

With the opening of the Fall semester, I went to the little town of Westerville, Ohio, where the University was located, and at once I began to teach. I received fifty cents a lesson. At first, my father had to subsidize me; soon I was earning enough to pay for my room and board. My mother's remark had aroused in me a sense of responsibility I had never known before. I was not a student; I was a member of the faculty. My youthfulness was a liability; not an asset. The life-long habit of prayer strengthened my will. I *would* be a successful teacher!

For my lodging, it had been arranged that I was to rent

the town's ice cream parlor, closed for the winter by the proprietors, Mr. and Mrs. Dibbs, who—as I recognized—had tried to make the place comfortable. With the ice cream tables removed, it looked denuded and bleak. In a curtained alcove there was room for a narrow bed, a bureau of sorts, a washstand and slop-jar. There was no closet, but fastened to the wall was a narrow strip of wood in which hooks had been inserted whereon I could hang my clothes. The worn ingrain carpet was depressing, in spite of its pattern of huge red roses faded into a background of green. The most prominent object in the room was a tall stove, for which I was supplied with a bucket of coal each day. If I wished hot water, I could heat it on my stove or go down to Mrs. Dibbs' kitchen. The room was lighted by oil-burning lamps. There were no toilet facilities in the house.

I took my meals next door. Here was a different atmosphere. The quiet, capable woman who ran the boardinghouse was one of the town's most prominent citizens. She owned and operated a dry goods store, and she became one of my staunchest friends. I could go to her with my small troubles and profit by her excellent advice. We learned to love each other. She is one of my Saints. For, because of my father's prominence, every move I made was watched and criticized; not by the faculty, but by gossipy women of the town, and . . . or, should I include the men?

The "Conservatory of Music" had once been a two-story dwelling with many-paned windows upstairs and down. It was at the end of College Avenue, a street of beauty, adorned on both sides by large shade-trees and by well-kept lawns in front of substantial dwellings. It was in this converted dwelling that I taught. It was a happy experience. It was, I believe, the happiest year of my life before I met my husband. Many of my men-students were older than I. It was gratifying to hear them learn to sing; their diction improve. They even gained a new self-confidence. I felt ashamed to accept their payments. Many of them were working their way through college; but had I offered free lessons, the relationship between teacher and student would no longer exist. They would have refused my offer.

The girl students were more difficult. One pupil born of German parents had a lovely clear soprano voice, but no conception of the interpretation of a song. I was trying to teach her German Lieder. In exasperation I asked her: "Don't you ever *tired* when you sing?"

"Oh, no," she replied laconically. "I could sing all day and never get tired."

"Don't you ever *cry* when you sing?"

She looked at me in astonishment. "Why should I cry?"

I was trying to arouse her soul! How else can one interpret a great song! She should have heard Mme. Schumann-Heink sing Brahms' "Lullaby."

There was no mail-delivery in Westerville. I had to go to the post office for my mail. I had taken a box. One morning, five or six of the younger students were leaning nonchalantly against the hitching-rail as I went for my mail. A small pasteboard box, neatly tied, was in my box; and with no little curiosity I opened it directly in front of the students. The box was full of very animated cockroaches. Of *course* I screamed! I had just enough presence of mind not to cast a glance at the pranksters. I regained my dignity and marched ahead. But how their laughter followed me!

When the month of May ushered in some warm days, Mr. and Mrs. Dibbs required my lodging. The ice cream parlor was to function again. Mrs. Dibbs told me that I might have her "parlor" on the ground floor, warning me that I must be careful of her furniture, and above all to be especially careful of her "moquet" carpet, her most cherished possession.

The month of May can be as unpredictable as April. I was hardly settled in the downstairs room when a cold rain brought wintry chill into my apartment. There was no way to heat the room. At night the storm increased in fury. The trees with their burgeoning leaves clawed at my windows, as if seeking sanctuary. The cold wind entered through every crack and crevice, and chilled me to the marrow. I lifted the oil lamp out of its brass stand and set it on the floor beside my chair. It gave just enough heat to warm my congealed fingers, so I could resume writing.

Alack! I smelled something burning. Hastily I lifted the lamp. It had burned a hole—a small hole, but yet *a hole*, into the sacrosanct carpet! In spite of the storm, I put on a raincoat and hastened to report the disaster to Miss Coleman, the art teacher, whom I had learned to love. Fortunately she was at home. She found some fine wool yarn, packed a brush and some tubes of paint, donned an ulster, and accompanied me back to my room.

"I'll darn the hole and then paint it. Mrs. Dibbs will never know!"

She really did perform a miracle, but I felt guilty. I wrote my father that night and made a full confession. His reply expressed extreme indignation—not at me, but at my landlady. "If she ever makes trouble," he wrote, "I'll buy her a new carpet." I still felt that we had cheated. I should have confessed; and she should have had her new carpet!

Commencement week was just around the corner. The Trustees and their wives arrived; also, parents of graduating students. My pupils were practicing for the musical event of the year, the Commencement Concert. The "Conservatory" was a busy place.

One morning, after the Trustees and the visiting parents had arrived, I approached the Conservatory. On each small pane of glass in that many-windowed building, there fairly leaped for attention three initials in unbelievably brilliant yellow paint: S S S—"Susie's Singing School"! The cockroach boys had done it again!

CHAPTER VI

Marriage

Before the next year, my father died. President Sanders could guarantee a salary for my successor. I was needed at home.

On the outskirts of Dayton was a large insane asylum. In more recent years (and indubitably more *decent* years) it is known as a mental hospital. A lovely young girl, daughter of a resident official of this institution, bemoaned the fact that her father claimed he could not afford to pay for the "singing lessons" she so ardently desired. I offered to give her what help I could. Her father relented enough to drive her to my home on one of his frequent errands to town, and he would call for her on his return.

She came twice a week for her lesson. Only once did her father, who was a good father after all, explain that he could not call for her that day. It was a beautiful spring day. I accompanied her to the asylum, riding in Mother's surrey "with the fringe on top," drawn by Father's well-matched horses which were driven by our indispensable Negro, Sidney.

As we drew up before the main entrance to the institution, Jane declared, "Such a handsome young doctor has just joined the staff. You *must* meet him!"

She hurried inside the wide entrance and emerged in a few minutes with a very handsome, but obviously sulky young man in tow, his hand still marking the place in the book he had been reading. We talked for a few minutes. Before I left, his finger was no longer in the book. He said that a horse and buggy were at the disposal of the three staff doctors, and he asked if he might call upon me some evening when it was his turn to have the horse and buggy. His name was Everett Anderson MacDonald, and he called upon me whenever he was free to do so.

My mother and my brother met him and liked him. Indeed, they asked me one evening, "What are you going to do with that young doctor? He's superior to any suitor you've had before."

It was commencement time at Otterbein again. I was invited to sing at the annual concert, the main musical event of the college year. Because of my father's devoted service to Otterbein, I accepted the honor. Dr. MacDonald asked if he might attend that concert; I had no objection. I went several days ahead of the event. As Dr. MacDonald was on his way to the railroad station, he met my mother on the street. He had a great respect for her, but how could he remove his hat? He had a large box of flowers under one arm, he carried a suitcase, and from his mouth protruded a long cigar! In some way, Mother must have solved his dilemma.

The concert hall was crowded. I was given a round of applause when I came onto the stage. I sang a group of songs. I have forgotten what they were, with the exception of the last. It was *Darling Nellie Gray*. I remembered that the composer of that song was buried in the Westerville cemetery.

Oh! my poor Nellie Gray, they have taken you away,
And I'll never see my darling any more;
I am sitting by the river and I'm weeping all the day
For you've gone from the old Kentucky shore.

They told me there wasn't a dry eye in the audience.

The next morning, Dr. MacDonald asked me to walk with him to the cemetery—the only trysting-place the students had. It was a serene and lovely place. There was no feeling of death there. The tall old trees had grown young again, covered with the tender foliage of early June. The gravestones were hidden by shrubbery in bloom. Through the trees, from the shady spot where we sat, we saw a man working in bright sunshine in a field below, reaping his golden wheat.

It was there that Everett proposed to me. I had just broken off a long-distance engagement. I didn't want a suitor; I wanted a friend. Three months later I said "yes." We were married in September the following year.

Everett had won his appointment at the insane asylum because of his high grades at Miami University, Oxford, Ohio, and his equally high grades in Medical School at Cincinnati, Ohio. At the asylum, he had borrowed a thousand dollars at seven percent interest from a kindly elderly woman on the staff. The only money I possessed was a thousand dollar City Railroad bond. We paid off the loan.

Business at the dry goods store was at a perilously low ebb, but mother allowed us to take possession of a comfortable house in which to begin our married life. The house was in an undesirable quarter of Dayton. We called it Heaven. My husband had rented a small office near my family home. While working at his practice in his specialty (eye, ear, nose and throat), he supplemented his earnings by small fees from insurance examinations, traveling miles on a bicycle after office-hours. Then my brother married, and at his request we gave up our Heaven and went to live with my mother. Although Everett's practice gradually improved, he was still undergoing the strain of the insurance examinations. Caught in a heavy rain one chilly night, he became very ill of a kidney infection so severe that at the end of eight months' confinement to bed his doctor told me he could not live.

"I am sorry to tell you this," he said. "He will learn it from you, and it will hasten the end."

For a week I could not swallow food, but I used my all-too-apparent disability as an excuse to distract my husband's attention from himself to me. It worked both ways. As I regained control of myself, he said one day, "I haven't heard you sing. Go on down and let me hear you sing!"

I made my way downstairs to the "back parlor" by way of the sitting room. Mother and Cousin Loma, my father's niece, who was like another daughter in the family, were sitting there waiting for news.

"Everett has asked me to sing for him," I told them.

Tears began rolling down their cheeks. "Oh, how can you!" Mother exclaimed.

"Listen!" I begged, "I've a job to do and it isn't an easy one. I must have your help and God's. I can't do it alone. If I don't sing when he asks me to, he will worry."

And so, I sang. And when I returned upstairs, Everett's look of worry had passed, and he had fallen quietly asleep. He knew nothing of the doctor's dire pronouncement until a year later. With the exception of two weeks when Mother provided a nurse for him, as a birthday present, and the woman who gave him a mild massage every night, I had taken entire care of him.

Another psysician was called into consultation. Upon his advice, we came to California. Mother had rented a small furnished house in Los Angeles; but like those Hebrew leaders in the Old Testament, guidance came to us. My brother wrote, "I am told that Redlands, California, is the best place for you." We were given the same advice by friends we had made at the small hotel where we were staying. Mother and Cousin Loma went to Redlands to verify the claims made for the small city. Mother cancelled her rental of the house in Los Angeles and rented another in Redlands. Within eight months my husband had recovered his health, had opened an office, and was at once busy. He was the only high-grade man in his specialty in this area.

Those were the days when the mountains stood majestic and awe-inspiring against a clear blue sky. We loved the orange groves; we loved the friendly people; we loved Redlands.

Business improved at the Dayton store. Mother built a handsome house in Redlands. At her death, Everett and I bought my brother's share in the house, and there we lived for twenty-seven years.

CHAPTER VII

The Automobile

Cal. veg. No. 911 (1905)
Cal. veg. No. 4431 (1906)

Everett was one of the first residents of Redlands to buy an automobile. It widened our horizon; we could explore the country. In 1905—over half a century ago!—we had an especially memorable trip.

The year before, we had driven up into the mountains near the foothills on which our beautiful city of Redlands is situated; and there, above the clouds, among the pines, we dwelt in perpetual sunshine and drank deep draughts of crisp, cold, pine-scented air.

Since then, we had come into the possession of a motor car; not a big touring car, but a Stevens-Duryea powerful enough to carry the two of us anywhere we might desire to go. For that year's outing we chose to go to Oceanside, a little known beach between Los Angeles and San Diego.

As the roads leading thither were scarcely more than trails, very different from Eastern highways—signposts being rarely seen—and as they were unknown to us, we ran such risk of losing our way over the seventy-five miles between Redlands and Oceanside that we determined to get an early start and allow a long day for possible detours.

If the doubting Easterner could have been with us that July morning, as at six o'clock we whirled out of Redlands, he must have relinquished his last atom of prejudice against our summer climate. The air was like wine, and so cool that I buttoned my heavy cloak about me.

Our way took us down the long winding grade into the San Timateo canyon. It is cause for congratulation when we have passed up or down one of these long, steep grades without seeing any sign of life. The Moreno grade winds up through a narrow pass to the summit of the mountain range which divides the two valleys. The road crosses back and forth, up and down, and back and forth, until the top is reached. Then it winds the other side, back and forth in the same manner, to the floor of the marvellous Moreno valley.

Surrounded on all sides by mountains, here brown and rugged in the foreground, there melting into soft purple in the distance, lies this level valley, like the emptied bed of some great lake. It is no wonder that some years ago men went mad over it and invested in its fertile soil all of their fortunes, only to find that with all of its fatal beauty it lacked the vital element, water. Abandonment and desolation! One could not imagine a drearier picture. Here at four corners were the typical brick buildings of a "boom" town, the foundations of a city, but with shattered windows and sinking walls that tell a tale of disaster. If only some magician could turn a stream of water through that beautiful valley, what wealth would be there, and how splendidly would the wildest dreams of the boom-period speculators be realized!

Sweeping around a sharp curve we came upon a herd of sheep grazing on the scanty pasture, the only sign of life in that wide region. And there we met our first problem of roads. Stretched out upon the plain before us, like the imprint of a gigantic hand, lay five roads, any one of which might lead us to our first goal, Temecula, or to our undoing.

Our carefully-studied map gave little help. We were about to choose as the children do: "My mother says I shall take this one," when there was a rattle of wheels and the faint murmur of a voice assuming definiteness in a stream of profanity as the owner of the voice drew nearer. A little old man, in a little old wagon, was driving a little old horse, to which he addressed a constant flow of such frightful oaths that they made my flesh creep.

It evidently was in a spirit of companionship between himself and his beast that he swore, for he uttered even his most terrible oaths in a mild, monotonous tone, which ceased suddenly as he saw our machine, and Everett walking toward him with a sign to halt.

Our inquiry as to direction unloosed another flood of volubility, less profane, the purport of which was that he was on his way to the post office, but that if we would proceed to his house, about a mile distant, he would overtake us and show us our way.

The idea of that forlorn horse overtaking our machine was ludicrous in the extreme, but he plodded off in one direction, while we flew away in another on high speed.

In a few minutes we came in sight of what we judged to be the old man's house, at some distance from the road; but, thinking we might economize time by learning the right way to Temecula at once, we turned in at the rickety gate and drove up to the barn.

A Mexican lad who gazed with awe-stricken eyes at the machine was the only human being within call, and he could speak no English. After wasting ten or fifteen minutes in that vain endeavor, we retraced our way and pushed ahead, trusting to luck that we should be on the right road.

A few miles brought us to a grade leading over into the next valley. Words fail to describe the vastness of that landscape and the rugged, desolate beauty of it.

On our way down the opposite side of the grade a large animal ran across our path, and up into the rocks, where he proceeded slowly, looking back with that curiosity which the unusual seems to excite in all wild animals. At first we thought he was a wildcat, but immediately, with a strange thrill, we realized that he was nothing less than a mountain lion, his long, thin legs, sharp ears and long, slender tail proving his identity. He ran so slowly that Everett might have shot him, but to our intense regret our only weapon was a small pocket revolver.

That brief excitement over, we settled back into our enjoyment of the scene and our constant wonder as to where we were going, a question that soon answered itself as we came into a little town called Lakeview. Why such a name should be given to so absolutely waterless a hamlet is past finding out—unless the very lack was father to the name.

A pretentious hotel adorned the town of Lakeview, which consisted of little else but the general store and a livery stable. Its shirt-sleeved proprietor told us how to find our way, his advice being to follow any trail that would take us around the next range of mountains and there inquire our way again.

The road out of Lakeview took us through heavy sand; across broad grain fields and pasture-lands, where we saw horses, cattle, and pigs in great numbers, but never a human being; and on out into the Perris Valley, where it broadened into a hard, straight highway along which we flew for miles on the high speed.

We lost our way again, but a good-natured German set us right and we swept on through a wonderful country, now of level plains stretching miles and miles away into a purple distance, awaiting only the magic of water to make them rich in fruit and grain; and then up steep grades, through strange, rocky hills, and out into ever new valleys.

And never a passing team along the way, never a man in sight! House after house we approached, many of them well-built and surrounded by trees and shrubs—here at last we should see life, faces peeping at us from the windows—only to find windows broken, doors swinging on rusty hinges and the blight of abandonment over all.

At last even these remnants of life ceased to come into view and we began to ascend a narrow but good road up a wild and picturesque canyon. Coasting down the other side we passed great pasture lands and came to a little town nestled among the trees. This proved to be Murrietta instead of, as we had hoped, Temecula.

We had been told to avoid the Indian Reservation, Pala, and to go through the Rainbow Canyon, but here again we missed our way and before we saw any one to set us right we were fifteen miles from Temecula and well into the Pala Pass. We decided to go ahead, nevertheless, but not until after we had cooled our hot machine and refreshed ourselves with a little food; so we pulled up under a huge live-oak and for an hour enjoyed its shade. Car and passengers both were the better for the rest. All of the power of the machine was needed for the next ten miles, while the driver dared not relax his vigilance a second, so narrow, rugged, and tortuous was the road. We were again so fortunate as not to pass any teams on the way, though we went by several Indian dwellings, evidently built by the government.

The half-dressed and unkempt men, women, and children who scurried out to behold the unwonted spectacle of a motor car on their mountain road might have made a timid person long for the crowded streets of a city, but only the dogs ventured to address us. It was a source of wonder to us how they could live on such barren land, their dwellings being crowded on little, bare spaces between great rocks; but we learned afterward that the greater part of the reservation is a fertile and profitable ranch, and that we were on a spur of Smith Mountain, the wildest and most desolate part of that region.

If ascending the grade was difficult, the descent into Pala was infinitely more so, the road curving sharply every few yards around huge boulders that appeared ready to drop upon us at the slightest jar.

However, we were thankful for the wrong turn that had taken us that way, for it is not often one's good fortune to behold such wild beauty, and while the road required careful driving, at no time did we find it dangerous.

To our left a mountain came in sight on whose sides was

a huge, pink blotch. We learned afterward that this was an old lithia bed, and that a short distance away were found the beautiful new gems, the kunzites. In those gorges have been found tourmalines, beryls, aquamarines, and many other semi-precious stones. Riding through them in a motor car one is so struck by their wildness and desolation that it seems likely that even yet they have not begun to give up their secrets to curious man.

Indeed, such millions of miles away from civilization did we feel ourselves to be, it was with a shock of surprise we caught the flutter of the Red, White, and Blue in the distance.

We soon found ourselves in the center of Pala, in front of the "Store," an unprepossessing frame building from whose flagstaff Old Glory gave the only bit of color to the gray landscape.

Underneath the shade of the solitary tree at Pala were the men, horses, and dogs of a prospecting party. Of them we asked our way and were told that between us and our next goal, Bonsal, lay fifteen miles of sand, and that earlier that very day a motor car had turned back to Temecula after a vain effort to pass through the sand. This information was not encouraging, but it failed to diminish our faith in our good machine. It was with the thrill of a new adventure that we whirled through the apparently uninhabited rows of houses and proceeded down the narrow, winding road to the bed of the San Luis Rey River. The road was so hard and smooth for several miles we began to think the story about sand was a myth, but when we came out upon the river bottom we found sand enough to prove the verity of the tale.

At Bonsal we came upon hard roads again and swept on to Oceanside on the high speed, to the last but by no means the least grade of the trip, at whose summit we came out upon a broad mesa and caught a first glimpse of the sparkling Pacific.

A ride full of interest was the short one through the beautiful valley to El San Luis Rey Mission, where good

Father O'Keith delighted to show the restorations carried out by the Franciscans themselves, of adobe, just as the original structure was built.

Another trip full of charm was to the vast Santa Marguerita ranch, a single principality of 260,000 acres, eight times as large as the District of Columbia, and over which only the privileged dared hunt, and where we were tantalized by the sight of quail as thick as chickens in a poultry yard and almost as tame. But the quail season was not yet on and we were forced to content ourselves with doves.

On the return trip to Redlands, we were to retrace our way as far as Bonsal and there turn aside over the Red Mountain road to Rainbow Canyon, thence to Temecula, and from there on by the way we had come.

My husband stopped to inquire his way of a man who assured him we should encounter no sand worth mentioning, but we had not gone two miles on the new road until we came to the bed of the river and there lay sand before us, glistening white for half a mile. Everett tried to rush the car through, but in a moment the wheels were whirling around and around as futilely as though in water and the poor engine became so hot that there was nothing left to do but give it a chance to cool and then try, try again. We spread gunny-sacks under the wheels, which were buried far over the tires, but our endeavors attained such feeble results that in a short time we all were hot and tired—car, driver, and passenger.

Everett left me with the machine and a revolver while he trudged back for aid. His tramp of two miles through the hot sun to the man who had been so hopeful about the sand gave him ample time for reflection, and while not of a suspicious nature he began to suspect that there was method in the rancher's encouragement, and that he even then might be awaiting his return with the keen enjoyment of a man who has things in his own power. In the meantime, I was suffering agonies of fear, not knowing precisely of what I was afraid—stray Indians from the reservation, Mexicans from the vast ranches through which we were passing, the revolver which I bravely held but did not know how to use, or the very silence and loneliness that brooded over the scene. I walked back to the little rise which lay between us and the solid road we had traversed, and from its summit I could see the little barn two miles away, whence must come our aid. Ere long, through the still, clear air, I caught the sound of voices and could see the horses and big wagon, mere specks at first, but growing cheeringly larger.

Unlike most of the horses in that region these good beasts were not afraid of the machine and pulled us out of our trouble in a few minutes. At last we were on a firm foundation.

"How much do I owe you?" inquired Everett.

"Well," replied the rancher, "I never done this sort of thing but once before, and that fellow he gave me a dollar. Would you think a dollar was too much?"

I wondered why Everett seemed apologetic. He told me later how suspicious he had been.

CHAPTER VIII

Daisy and the Cocoanut

On this our first trip to the Island of Oahu we had the good fortune to find on board ship a colleague of Everett's, Dr. Humes Roberts, distinguished eye specialist of Pasadena, and his charming wife, Juliet.

We were a congenial quartette and we toured the island together. So, when we were told that one of the most interesting sights on Oahu was to see Daisy, the huge African elephant, take an unpeeled cocoanut in her trunk, peel off the outer husk, crush the inner shell, and drink the cocoanut milk with an ecstatic expression, we hired a drive-your-own car, bought a supply of unshelled cocoanuts and drove to the scene of Daisy's captivity.

While the two doctors were adjusting their cameras, impulsively, as always, I picked up a cocoanut, stooped under the heavy rope which confined the area and ran toward the huge pachyderm. I did not know that the heavy rope was to prevent people from entering that area, nor was I aware of the difference in temperament between the African and the Indian elephants. I thought all elephants were friendly creatures; and when I was near enough to Daisy, I tossed her my cocoanut.

It fell short, and as I moved forward to retrieve it and practically hand it to her, she let out a roar of rage and lunged at me, her trunk missing me by a few inches. Fortunately for me, she was heavily chained, another fact I had not observed in my foolish eagerness.

I was still not aware of the horrible death I had just escaped until I saw my husband's stricken face. Our friends too had a look of horror. A busload of natives had halted nearby, and in their native tongue they jabbered a scolding.

Daisy killed her keeper not long after this incident. She was too great a menace to be allowed to live and she was shot to death.

The absurdity of my being almost killed by an elephant on the Elysian island of Oahu was too good a story to keep —too good, that is, until I saw what it did to my husband.

Daisy was not mentioned again.

CHAPTER IX

The War Years: "Uncle Henry"

The year was 1918 and our nation was at war. A group of patriotic women of Redlands, under the leadership of Mabel Cameron, rented an empty store-room downtown and sent out a call for contributions of any sort: discarded clothing, old furniture, books, pictures, any article that might be salable, salvaged from cobwebby attic corners. The women wore white uniforms with a Red Cross symbol. The shop was known as the Red Cross Shop.

The response was so immediate and generous that the fame of it spread rapidly. Mrs. Cameron was called to many surrounding communities to explain how her method worked. Somewhere I have a photograph of those dedicated women; many of them have died long since, while I live on and on.

What part could I take thirty-eight years ago, confined as I was to bed? My imagination caught fire. I wrote some "propaganda-pieces" and sent them to the editor of *The Redlands Daily Facts*. I signed the "pieces" *Uncle Henry*. No one suspected who "Uncle Henry" was, but his "pieces" achieved an astonishing result. I had forgotten completely these "Uncle Henry" pieces. I found them, yellowed with age, in an attic trunk. A few of them may find a place in *The Backward Look*.

ARE YOU HURT ENOUGH?

EDITOR FACTS:
I was sitting in the back part of my store yesterday;
It was early afternoon and business was dull,
And I was about half asleep.
I didn't see anyone come in at the door
But all of a sudden there was a crowd
Of young fellows in khaki
Looking at me.
One of them came close to me and asked—
With his bright eyes boring into me,
"How much did you give for us?"
"For you?" said I. "I don't quite get you."
"Oh, yes you do!" he said.
"Oh, do you mean for the Red Cross War Fund?"
    I asked.
"Well, I can't see that it's any of your business!"
With that they all crowded up around me.
"How much did you give for us?" they asked,
Whispering all together.
"Well," I said, trying to bluster a little,
But feeling all at once, kind of mean and small,
"Well, if you mean the War Fund, I gave a few
    good dollars;
And I tell you chaps that what with taxes and
    gasoline,
And this, that and the other,
It was all I could afford."
And what I said sounded so familiar and sensible
That I got to be good friends with myself again.
But the young man that spoke first,
He was a fine, straight, clean-looking boy—
He said, "Now then, boys, let's show this man
What we're expected to give for him."
I don't know what happened, but the next minute
I was with those boys somewhere out in Hell!

And they were being dragged out of trenches,
Mangled wrecks of boys!
Begging they were and crying for aid, for Red Cross
aid,
For *my* aid!
The young chap who had talked to me had an arm
And part of a shoulder shot away.
He looked up at me and I had to lean over him and
hear him say,
"You are comfortable . . . and easy.
You want to take a little summer trip and buy a
new auto.
You've hung flags . . . on your front porch . . .
And on your car . . . and you've given a few good
dollars . . .
And . . . Oh, God! This . . . is what
You expect us others . . . to do . . . for you!"
It was a dream,
But I want to say, Mr. Editor,
That I woke up with sweat rolling down my face
And the sweat was cold!
I went out like Judas did, but I didn't hang myself.
I went out and pledged two hundred dollars to
The Red Cross War Fund.
And my only fear is, that even at that I am not
Going to be hurt enough!

—UNCLE HENRY

REDLANDS HAS SURE BEEN HOT!

EDITOR FACTS:
It's funny, how different people take it;
To hear some of 'em complain
You'd think they had all the heat
Turned on inside of 'emselves
Like an electric iron,

And suffering something awful.
And there's others that just seem to shed it
Like asbestos.
My neighbor, he's the asbestos kind.
He was saying on Sunday
That mighty few of us really suffer
With heat.
"We just get mighty uncomfortable," he says,
"And we can't get away from what's making us
      uncomfortable,
And that gets our goat and we fuss!
It makes me think," he said,
"About those fellows in the trenches
That get shot up.
They're really suffering, suffering tortures
That you and I can't even think about;
Lots of our own boys are going to suffer
Like that,
And they can't get away from it
Unless we help.
The thermometer goes up to 114
And we think we're killed and send a hurry-call
      for ice cream
And any other kind of first-aid that's got ice
      in it!"
My neighbor just kind of sucked in his
      breath . . .
And said,
"Well, there's some of us that won't sit around
Drinking ice-cream sodas,
And let those poor boys die
Because their nurse didn't have any bandages
To keep 'em from bleeding to death!"
. . . Somehow, my neighbor makes me feel
As if it was up to him and me.
I'm going to quit talking to him

Or else . . . say, I wonder how Redlands is
    coming through
With that $25,000?

                      —UNCLE HENRY

JOEY GIVES A LESSON

EDITOR FACTS:
One night before school closed I said,
"Let's go to the movies and see
What Charley Chaplin's up to now."
The wife, she agreed that t'would
Be fine; but our boy, Joey, he squirmed
This way and that, and then he said,
"Would you just as lief give me
The money for my ticket, and let
Me stay at home?" Say! He's such
A fan for the movies, I just sat
And stared at him; and then I says,
"What's biting you, son?"
Well, he turned red and was all
Fussed up; but finally I got it out
Of him that he wanted to save
That money for Thrift Stamps!
Now what do you know about that!
He said all the other kids were signing up,
And that the big fellows who could work,
Like the High School boys,
They were pledging twenty plunks!
"Every man, woman, and child," he says,
Like he's speaking a piece,
"Is asked to save that much."
"Joey," I says, "what do you want
The Thrift Stamps for? Are you
Aiming to be rich some day?"
He looked straight up at me
Kind of wide-eyed and serious.

"Why, Dad," he says, "even us kids
Have got to help
Lick the Kaiser!"
Can you beat it? Those kids
Learning to value money not for what
It'll buy them, but to help
Make this a better world.

*   *   *

The wife and I didn't go to the movies either.
Joey, he'd given us something
To think about.

—UNCLE HENRY

AND SO HAVE YOU

EDITOR FACTS:
I was over having a smoke on my neighbor's porch
Last night. I'd noticed that he'd not been
Smoking here of late. I meant to ask him "Why?"
But Tom Slim rolled along in his auto.
He'd had it painted, and a new top put on,
With plate-glass port-holes all around.
He saw us and stopped beside the curb.
"She's lookin' pretty classy, ain't she, boys?"
He said, "Ran her down to the beach and back
On Sunday. Some car! I'm going to take
The folks for a spin to San Diego, Saturday."
My neighbor rubbed his finger along the rim
Of Tom's new tire. "I suppose," he said,
"You've pledged the limit of War Stamps."
Tom's grin faded. He got the look
Of a man who goes away inside
Of himself and shuts the door.
"Of course," he said, reaching for his starter,
"I'll sign up for what I can. But we've cut down
Expenses to rock bottom as it is. Old Hi Cost
Puts the crimp into War Stamps so far as I'm

Concerned. Well, I've got to be moving."
Tom had his engine turning over pretty fast,
But my neighbor hung over the car-door.
"Those pleasure rides," he says, "don't they cost
A lot of War Stamps?"
"A man's got to live his own life!"
Tom flung back. Say, isn't it funny?
That's what I'd been telling myself, right along;
But when I heard another man say it
It sounded pretty small.
"900,000 of our boys," my neighbor said, "with
    the best
Of life before them, are already Over There
Linking arms with death, just to ram it home
That *'No man liveth unto himself.'*
We've had our peaceful chance at life
And we're not called upon to go; but thank God!
The government lets every he-man, and every
Woman and child in on the job!
The war-saver over here becomes
A savior Over There."
After Tom had gone I said to my neighbor,
"How come you're not smoking any more?"
He got as red as any girl. "Oh," he says,
Kind of casual, "I've got a pretty stiff
Obligation to meet."
And away back in my brain something keeps urging:
"So have YOU!"

—UNCLE HENRY

For Self-Sacrifice Week, this appeal appeared in *The Redlands Daily Facts* under the heading "Red Cross Notes":

SELF-SACRIFICE WEEK

Our boys are sacrificing life itself for us. What will we sacrifice for them?

To the men, women and children of Redlands:
Bring to the Red Cross Shop this week something of
value, that represents sacrifice on your part.

THEY WHO WERE WISE-HEARTED
(Exodus 35:20–30)

In the sacred word is written
    how the Israelites of old,
When the need was laid upon them
    brought their offerings of gold,
Of silver and fine linen,
    a vast treasure—we are told—
      To carry on the work.

"Every one that was wise-hearted"—
    so the noble record reads
(It has echoed down the ages
    and survived a thousand creeds),
Made his sacrifices gladly,
    put aside his selfish greeds,
      To carry on the work.

The gifts themselves have crumbled
    into dust long, long ago,
For the years have passed by thousands,
    and Time grinds fine and slow;
But the ancient shining sacrifice
    with light is still aglow—
      They carried on the work!

You and I are making a new record,
    now, today!
We ar writing, writing, writing,
    what will never fade away;
Are you one of the wise-hearted
    who—the histories will say—
      Have carried on the work?

Your little dear possession,
    at a breath it disappears;
But the part that you are playing
    lives undying down the years;
For America is YOU
    will you heed the call She hears,
        And carry on the work?

Epilogue

The Backward Look is now the Forward Look.

"For once you were darkness,
But now you are light;
Walk as children of light,
For the fruit of light is found
In all that is good and right and true." (Ephesians 5:8,9)

SUSANNE RIKE MACDONALD